VENICE

A journey through
the art, history and architectural masterpieces
of the most beautiful city in the world.

CONTENTS

THE GRAND CANAL ITS PALACES
Page 6

The origins of Venice are lost in legend. According to the most credited version, the first settlements in the islands in the lagoon date back to the 6th-7th centuries when the Lombard invasions of the Venetian plains prompted the people on the coast to move to a place that could be more easily defended. Others maintain that Venice had already been a Roman city and port for some time. Until about 800, other centres, like Grado and Aquileia, had held the political and territorial control of the Lagoon. It was only due to a series of fortunate coincidences that the symbols of Byzantine political authority and those of the religious authority become concentrated in Venice in the early 11th century. Around 810, the doge (from the Latin "dux", commander), the highest representative of the Byzantine Empire, moved to Rivoalto, the oldest nucleus of Venice, today known as Rialto. In 828, two merchants brought the body of St. Mark, who became the patron saint of the city, to the islands. The winged lion, the symbol of the saint, became the emblem of the state. Having reached political and religious pre-eminence, Venice established an astute system of alliances to protect herself from external aggression. She then gave herself a solid, Republican type government, based on the Greater Council, made up of members from the most influential noble families. In the 13th century, Venice extended her control to Dalmatia and started a war with Genoa which lasted for more than a century. This was the start of a period that was also marked by conflict with the Viscontis, the dukes of Milan, and the fearful Black Plague, which in 1348 decimated the population by half. The crisis was only temporary because in the 15th century the fate of the city on the lagoon improved and it reached its greatest splendour. Venice controlled the whole of the Adriatic, as far as the Peloponnese and began to conquer territories on the mainland. The expansionism of the Serenissima (as the republic was named) came to a standstill in 1509 after the defeat of Agnadello by the league of Cambrai, an alliance by the most important Italian and European states that had rushed to support the Papacy, which intended to defend its territories in Romagna from Venice's expansionist aims. The defeat jeopardised the very existence of the Venetian state, triggering off a series of uprisings which were quelled only with difficulty. The narrowly escaped danger suggested a more cautious policy, which lasted for almost two centuries, guaranteeing peace and prosperity for the city. This was the Venetian Renaissance, in which the Serenissima was a protagonist of the arts and sciences like Rome and Florence. However, the conflict against the Turks continued and, despite the victory at Lepanto in 1571 and regaining Morea and Athens at the end of the 17th century, weakened Venice from the financial point of view. Independence remained, but the Serenissima was deprived of it by Napoleon, who ceded the Venetian territories to the Habsburg Empire of Austria, with the treaty of Campoformio in 1797, effectively putting an end to a long autonomy. Venice was then annexed to the Kingdom of Italy in 1866. The "geographical" isolation of the city also came to an end in the same period: it was attached to the mainland in 1846 by the railway bridge, which in 1932 also became a road. Today Venice continues to delight the world, thanks to new architectural additions, like the extraordinary Ponte della Costituzione (Bridge of the Constitution) designed by the Spanish architect Santiago Calatrava, which crosses the Grand Canal between Piazzale Roma and the railway station of Venice Santa Lucia. However, the city also has to deal with the phenomenon of high water in the Lagoon and the subsiding of the land on which it is built, which threaten its very survival. To save the city, the grandiose "Moses" system of locks is being built, which aims to regulate the tides in the Lagoon and will be completed in 2012.

THE GRAND CANAL
ITS PALACES

Four kilometres of water between splendid palaces. The Grand Canal, affectionately called the "Canalazzo" is the main thoroughfare of Venice: at its deepest it is 5 metres deep and, on average, it is 50 metres wide. It follows a course like a backward-shaped S which starts from the railway station of Santa Lucia and ends at the Punta della Dogana, opposite St. Mark's Square. You can travel down the Grand Canal by vaporetto, on one of the many lines that cross it. On the other hand, it is impossible to follow it on foot, as the streets in Venice do not follow the waterways.

The only way to admire the finest Venetian palaces and their sumpt-

On the left, Palazzo Calbo-Crotta, where the white awnings are, and the dome of the

Palazzo Barbarigo.

church of St. Jeremy can be seen.

uous façades is therefore by water. Starting from the station, you pass immediately under the white stone **Ponte degli Scalzi**, at the foot of which, looking towards the left, there is the church of the same name. The route can ideally be divided into three parts: from the station to the Rialto Bridge, the long straight stretch to Palazzo Mocenigo, and the last curved part which ends opposite St. Mark's Square. In the first part, the **Fondaco dei Turchi** stands out on the right, close to the stop of San Marcuola. This is a long white building, flanked by two towers. In Venetian-Byzantine style, it is one of the oldest buildings in the city. Slightly further on, on the left, there is the large **Palazzo Vendramin-Calergi**, home in the

Palazzo Vendramin-Calergi.

winter to the Municipal Casino. Continuing, after the two large buildings of **Ca' Pesaro** and **Ca' Corner della Regina**, on the right, you can admire the splendid **Ca' d'Oro**, the finest building of Venetian floral gothic, evidence of a very refined art, by Bartolomeo Bon and Matteo Raverti. The long structures of the Fabbriche Nuove and of the Fabbriche Vecchie, on the right, announce that we are near the Rialto Bridge. After passing under the bridge, you enter the stretch of the richest palaces, those of the wealthiest families of Venice, such as the **Palazzo Loredan** and **Palazzo Farsetti**, medieval buildings in the Byzantine style. Further on, **Palazzo Grimani** appears, a sixteenth-century building by Sanmicheli. When the Canal begins to bend towards the left, there appear some very famous buildings, such as **Ca' Foscari**, the university of Venice, in the gothic style, and **Palazzo Giustinian**, where Wagner stayed between 1858 and 1859, when he composed *Tristan und Isolde*. On the opposite side, on the left, there stands **Palazzo Grassi**, where major art exhibitions are

On the left, the corner of Palazzo dei Camerlenghi.

The Cà d'Oro.

held. Again on the left, for those going towards St. Mark's, **Palazzo Cavalli Franchetti** and then **Palazzo Corner called Ca' Granda**, designed by Jacopo Sansovino, can be seen. There then appears the dome of Santa Maria della Salute, on the right, which announces that you will soon be leaving the Grand Canal.

Palazzo Cavalli-Franchetti.

THE *R*IALTO BRIDGE

At first it was a simple pontoon bridge laid out in around 1172 to allow crossing the Grand Canal. Until then, to get from one side to the other was only possible by boat.

The Rialto Bridge was thus the first bridge in Venice. Then, between 1200 and 1260, the simple floating walkway was

A view from the Riva del Vin, just under the Rialto Bridge.

replaced by a real suspended wooden structure.

Subsequently, after it had collapsed three times, the last time in 1524, the governor of the Serenissima decided to make the Rialto bridge the first stone bridge in the city. A competition was announced, with important fig-

ures such as Palladio, Vignola, Sansovino and Michelangelo taking part.

Curious enough, it was the architect Antonio Da Ponte who won. Building the bridge was no easy feat.

The subsiding soil and the complexity of the project set quite a few problems.

The bridge is 28 metres long, with only one span and at the midpoint

is 7.5 metres above the level of the water, which was sufficient to allow the passage of the Venetian galleys and the large vessel of the Doge, the Bucintoro, used on important celebrations. The work to complete the bridge lasted from 1588 to 1591. The two rows of shops on the bridge were added at a later stage.

The bridge was completely restored in 1977.

$\mathscr{A}$CADEMY
OF FINE ARTS

The richest collection of Venetian art is in the **Galleries of the Academy**, which look on to Campo della Carità, one of the loveliest squares in the city (in the local dialect, "campo" means square).

From the Grand Canal you can see the Academy which is close to the wooden bridge of the same name, a slender footbridge that is near the end of the canal, not far from the Punta della Dogana. The en-

The entrance to the Galleries of the Academy, in Campo della Carità, on the Grand Canal

Bellini - Sacred Conversation

trance is in the white building which was once the School of Santa Maria della Carità and the convent of the Canonici Lateranensi, built by Palladio in 1560. The premises of the monks and the nearby Church of La Carità have been the Academy since 1817. The collection consists of an original nucleus, formerly owned by the Republic of the Serenissima, to which donations by private individuals have been added. All the greatest representatives of Venetian painting are represented in the collection: Paolo and Lorenzo Veneziano, Michele Giambono, Giovanni Bellini and Vittore Carpaccio for the 14th and 15th centuries; Giorgione, Tiziano, Tintoretto, Veronese, Bassano and Lorenzo Lotto for the 16th century; Tiepolo, Giambattista Piazzetta, Longhi and Rosalba Carriera for the

Carpaccio – Apotheosis of St. Ursula.

17th and 18th centuries. There is of course a series of sketches by Antonio Canal, known as Canaletto, the artist who with his landscapes made Venice famous all

Lotto – Portrait of a young gentleman.

over the world. The collection is completed by some folios by Leonardo da Vinci. The finest works include the cycle of paintings of the *Legend of St. Ursula* by Carpaccio, made up of nine canvases painted by the master between 1490 and 1496. *The Presentation of the Virgin at the Temple* by Tiziano is an example of narrative painting which tells, through images, a story or episode. It is a grandiose composition, which represents the masterpiece

Canaletto – Porch

Tiziano - Presentation of the Virgin at the Temple.

Tintoretto – St. Mark frees a slave.

of the full artistic maturity of the painter. Again by Tiziano, we can admire *La Pietà*, his last and unfinished work, of 1576, the year the artist died of the plague.

Tiepolo – The rape of Europa.

Tiziano – St. John the Baptist.

THE PALAZZO VENIER DEI LEONI
"THE GUGGENHEIM FOUNDATION"

In the district of Dorsoduro, halfway between the Academy and the Church of Santa Maria della Salute, there is a low white 18th century building, Palazzo Venier dei Leoni, which holds one of the most particular collections of art in Venice.

This is the **Peggy Guggenheim Foundation**, named after the great American collector, granddaughter of the millionaire Solomon Guggenheim and wife of the artist Max Ernst. The first collection she created was that of the famous Guggenheim Museum

A view of the final stretch of the Grand Canal, on to which Palazzo Venier dei Leoni,

Palazzo Venier dei Leoni seen from the Grand Canal.

in New York, inaugurated in 1942. Then, in 1948, Peggy bought Palazzo Venier dei Leoni and the year afterwards opened it to visitors as a museum of modern art. The pictures in it reflect the rich collector's taste in art. There are Surrealist works and avant-garde paintings from the early 20th century. The best known signatures include Mondrian, Klee, Balla, Severini, De Chirico, Picasso, Max Ernst, Mirò and the American Jackson Pollock.

on the right, looks.

De Chirico – The red tower.

PUNTA DELLA DOGANA

An aerial view of the Punta della Dogana, with the white tower designed by Giuseppe Benoni.

The tip of land that extends along the right of the Grand Canal towards the Lagoon is a perfect point to admire St. Mark's Basin and the Doges' Palace. It takes the name of Punta della Dogana, because this is where there was one of the two customs ("dogana") of Venice, that of the sea, where the goods from all the vessels coming from outside the Lagoon were checked. The other customs, that "of the land" was near the Rialto Bridge. The customs house was built between 1677 and 1682 by the architect Giuseppe Benoni, who won a competition. A small white tower dominates the complex. At its top, some bronze statues support a golden sphere, on which the stat- ue of *Fortune*, by the artist Bernardo Falcone, is balanced. In the past, the Punta della Dogana was called the Punta della Trinità, in tribute to the church, the monastery and the school that stood there. Another name used to indicate this place is Punta del Sale.

The tower of the Dogana.

$\mathscr{S}$t. Mark's Basin

The busiest stretch of sea in Venice, crowded with gondolas, the landing stages of the vaporettos and where the larger vessels would

Arriving in the Basin.

be moored, is the basin facing St. Mark's Square. Its eastern boundary is the Riva degli Schiavoni and the district of Castello, on the south there is the island of San Giorgio Maggiore and on the west the entrance to the Grand Canal. Leaving the Grand Canal by vaporetto, before admiring the Doges' Palace, you can see the low building of Harry's Bar, Venice's most famous café and restaurant

in the world. The **Palazzo del Magistrato** then appears, with its low arcades, and the **Royal Gardens**, which Napoleon wanted and obtained from the demolition of the four huge buildings of the granaries of Terranova, which in the 14th century, when they were built, were the largest grain stores in Europe.

It was also for this reason that the basin of St. Mark was the commercial and not just political centre of Venice. Alongside the Royal Gardens there is the massive and square building of the **Mint**, where the Venetian currency, the "zecchino" was produced (called ducat until the middle of the 16th century). It was accepted practically

An aerial view of St. Mark's Basin.

throughout Europe, making it a real international currency. The present-day Palace of the Mint was built to a design by Sansovino in the 16th century. Behind the Mint there stands out the **Bell Tower,** which the Venetians call the "paròn de casa" (lord of the house). At its side can be seen, with St. Mark's Square in the background, the **Clock Tower**

The Bell Tower dominates the Basin.

and, on its right, **St. Mark's Basilica.** Continuing on the water, the profile of the **Doges' Palace** passes by, with its finely decorated façade, and then the famous **Bridge of Sighs**, which links the Doges' Palace with the Prisons. A curiosity: once the square in front of the Doges' Palace did not exist and the sea came as far as the front of St. Mark's Basilica. It was filled in with earth in the 12th century.

The Bell Tower, in the foreground, and in the background the Basilica of St. Mark.

Although it has always been the throbbing heart of Venice, St. Mark's Square has changed appearance several times. The architecture is the result of much work. Until the 14th century, the backdrop was exclusively **St. Mark's Basilica**, built of bricks and much "poorer" than it is today, and the **Doges' Palace**, which looked more like a castle than an elegant government building.

The Clock Tower.

The **Bell Tower** was a high tower, without the spire. Of the buildings of the **Procuratie**, which close the square in front of the Basilica, there only existed the "**Vecchie**", which at that time had a far less refined architecture. The Doges' Palace began to take on its present-day appearance after a number of alterations begun in the 15th century. The total renovation of the square was then entrusted to the architect

The two Moors above the Clock Tower.

Jacopo Tatti from 1529 onwards. He is better known as Sansovino and worked on the square for over thirty years. He restored the Procuratie Vecchie, the Basilica and the Bell Tower, built the **Mint** and started the work on the nearby **Libreria**. This was completed at a later date

The Libreria by Sansovino.

An aerial view of the square.

by Vincenzo Scamozzi, to whom we also owe the design of the **Procuratíe Nuove**, which was to house the Procurators of St. Mark. Today, under the porticos of the Procuratíe there are prestigious cafés, where tourists can fully enjoy the unique sight of the square in complete relaxation. The Florian and Quadri cafés are the best known. The short side of the square is closed by a building, called the **Ala Napoleonica**, built in the early 19th century. Today it houses the *Correr Museum* or the museum of *Venetian Civilization,* with a wealth of paintings and sculptures. On the northern side, the square is closed by the **Clock Tower**, a Renaissance building at the top of which there is a terrace with a bell struck by two figures. They are called the Moors due to the dark patina that the bronze in which they are sculpted has taken on. Further below, the enormous golden clock can be seen, by Giampaolo and Giancarlo Ranieri, which shows the times, the phases of the moon and the signs of the zodiac, which are useful for forecasting the movements of the tides.

The splendid golden façade of St. Mark's Basilica complies with the standards of

The great Venetian basilica is one of the most unusual churches in Christendom. It is greatly inspired, in its architecture and decoration,

oriental Byzantine art.

by oriental and Byzantine culture, of which Venice wanted to be the ambassador in the West. It is built to a Greek cross plan, with three naves, covered by a cluster of domes that give it an unmistakable appearance. The first construction of the church was decided in 828 when the remains of the Apostle Mark were brought from Alexandria in Egypt to Venice, but in 976 it was destroyed by fire and

The Last Judgement, the decoration of the central lunette of the façade, above the

rebuilt in 978. After 1000, it was demolished because considered inadequate and the present-day basilica dates back to the construction begun in 1063 by the doge Domenico Contarini. At first

A detail of the façade.

it was a very simple plain brick building and with the domes much lower than they are today. A series of alterations and additions, over a long time span between the 11th and the 15th centuries, transformed it completely. The domes were raised, with a wooden structure covered by lead for the roof. The façade was covered with exquisite marble and further decorated by a double row of chapiters. A series of Gothic-style decorations was positioned to crown the arches to give an upward movement to the massive church and harmonize it

main portal.

stylistically with the neighbouring Doges' Palace. However, what is most impressive about the exterior are the decorations on a gold background, typical of Byzantine art. The whole Basilica, seen from afar, shines in the sun's rays. Above the rich portal there are the famous *four horses,* the symbol of free Venice, taken from Constantinople by the doge Enrico Dandolo after the crusade of 1204 as war loot. Their origin is uncertain: some say they are the work of the sculptor Lysippos, active in ancient Greece in the 4th century BC. Venice lost them to Napoleon, who took them to Paris, but regained possession of them in 1815. They were recently replaced by bronze copies as restoration work was necessary on the orig-

inals, which can now be seen in the Museum of the Basilica. The aspect of wealth and ostentation on the outside is also found inside St. Mark's Basilica.

The golden background is dominant here as well, enriched by an incredible number of mosaics, covering 8,000 square metres. The mosaics on the walls, which had the purpose of teaching the Bible to the illiterate people, were completed over a long period of time, from the 11th to the 15th century. As the inside is not very well lit, these works of art are revealed only gradually, as the visit proceeds from the entrance towards the apse. In the basilica, the splendid mosaics of *Christ Pantocrator*, which is in the conch of the apse of St. Mark, the *Ascension*, in the largest dome at the junction of the central nave with the transept and of the

The four horses.

The interior of the Basilica, the central nave.

Pentecost in the central nave, can be admired.

The *Gold Altarpiece*, on the great altar, is an extremely refined piece of craftsmanship, in gold and silver, completed in the 10th century and later enriched with details until the 14th century.

Originally commissioned from

Christ Pantocrator.

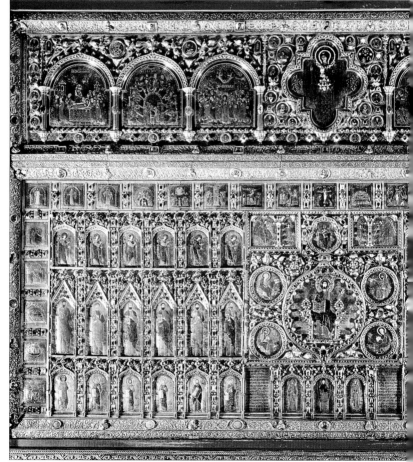

The Gold Altarpiece, studded with 1,927 precious stones and decorated with 80 polychrome

artists in Constantinople, its greatest splendour is due to the work of Giampaolo Boninsegna in 1345. The polychrome marble *floors*, laid in the 12th century according to techniques developed by the Romans, are also very fine. At the back of the Basilica, the iconostasis, a fine balustrade in rare red mar-

A detail of the mosaic: The discovery of the relics of St. Mark.

bles, separates the raised area of the choir under which there is the crypt. This underground part, completed in the 11th century, held the remains of St. Mark, which had been found in a pillar of the previous basilica.

Of great interest is the visit to the *Treasure of St. Mark,* a rich collection of icons and sacred vestments brought to Venice after the Crusade of 1204 and the numerous expeditions in ancient times.

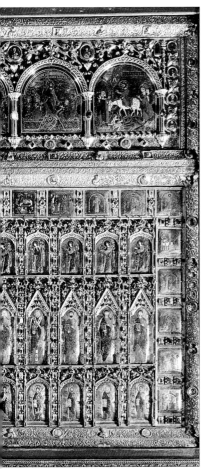

enamels showing Gospel scenes.

A detail of the interior.

THE $\mathcal{D}$OGES' PALACE

More beautiful than the residence of a king, more elegant than a work of art, more famous than the best known of monuments. The Doges' Palace in Venice is one of the best known buildings in the world, a masterpiece of harmony and grace, the symbol of political power and

The south-western corner of the Doges' Palace on a high water day.

justice. And yet, to reach the final stage in which we can see it, the building also underwent many changes, renovations and additions. For the Venetians it has always been the symbol of the state: the residence of the Doge, the supreme leader of the city, the place where the government met and a court of law, where the fearsome Council of Ten sat, the court that in practice had the power of life and death over citizens. Looking at it from the outside, the

The Doges' Palace and, alongside, the Straw Bridge.

lightness of the Gothic architecture and the decoration mask the internal impressiveness of the structure, which has three floors, where there was space for all the most important offices that ran the Venetian Republic. Initially, earlier than 1000, the palace must have looked like a fortress, a

Mediterranean and its seat of government had to express its strength, security and wealth. The changes concerned above all the two most visible wings of the building, the one looking out to sea and the one that looks on to the small square. They were rebuilt respectively in 1340 and 1423, not only with aesthetic taste, but also with great architectural expertise.

stronghold with a square plan defended by high walls and further protected on the side of the basin by massive towers. Between 1300 and 1500 however, major changes were made, also laid down by the new political climate. Venice no longer risked being besieged: it was now the greatest power in the

The light portico on the ground floor and the first floor gallery support the weight of the two upper floors. To be admired are the capitals of the columns, sculpted between the 14th and 15th centuries and the corner sculptures. Access to the interior is through the **Porta della Carta**, at the back

The Chamber of the Senate.

of the building, which opens, through the **Portico Foscari**, on to the refined internal courtyard.

Here you can admire the elegance of the eastern wing, designed by the architect Antonio Rizzo, the building of which started in 1485. Rizzo also designed the **Giants' Steps,** on which the doge was crowned, and which leads to the floor of the Loggias. On this level there are the offices of the different minor judiciaries: the "Avogaria", which prepared the cases for trial, the Chancellery, the Censors and the "Provveditori della Milizia da Mar", who fitted out the fleet's galleys. The Doge's apartments were on the first floor in the north-eastern part of the palace, reached through the splendid **Golden Staircase**, designed in 1538 by Sansovino for the doge Andrea Gritti, which owes its name to the vault decorated with golden stucco work. Completed in 1559 by Scarpagnino, this was the offi-

The Chamber of the Anticollege: Marriage of Bacchus and Ariadne by Tintoretto.

cial entrance, for the magistrates and visiting high dignitaries. Continuing to the first floor, you can get an idea of how the Republic of the Serenissima worked. Here there were the offices of various minor judiciaries and the **Chamber of the Great Council**, where the government met to take its decisions. A grandiose canvas stands out on the back wall, painted by Tintoretto between 1588 and 1590, showing *Paradise*. On the same floor there is also the **Chamber of the Ballot**, where the votes of the Great Council were counted. On the second floor, there are more richly decorated rooms: standing out in particular are the **Chamber of the Senate** with the splendid ceiling by Tintoretto and the **Chamber of the Council of Ten**, with paintings by Veronese.

Tintoretto – detail of Paradise.

Chamber of the Great Council.

THE *R*IVA DEGLI SCHIAVONI

The wide quay on the sea in front of the Doges' Palace, after passing the Straw Bridge, built in 1360, becomes a long promenade, the Riva degli Schiavoni, invaded every day by the stalls of street

Riva degli Schiavoni, the most picturesque and bustling place for a walk in Venice.

traders as well as a rich offer of shops and cafés and restaurants. It is 500 metres long and goes southwards, along the district of Castello, until it reaches the venue of the famous Biennale of Venice. It owes its name to the merchants

from Dalmatia, called Slavonia-Schiavonia in ancient times. Towards the end of the 18th century, the Senate developed it and widened it and it thus became one of the favourite places of Venetians for their walks. Just after the **Straw Bridge**, from which the **Bridge of Sighs** can be admired, you are in front of the old prisons. Continuing just a little way on, we come to the very famous Grand Hotel Danieli, a real institution. It has been open since 1822, when Giuseppe Dal Niel (who gave his name to the hotel) decided to adapt the historical palace, owned by the Dandolo family, to offer hospitality. All the most famous people who have visited Venice, from William of Prussia to Wagner, from Balzac to Proust, from Dickens to Debussy, stayed at the Danieli.

THE $\mathcal{B}$RIDGE OF SIGHS

There is not a tourist who has been to Venice who has not come to see it. And yet this small and elegant bridge is synonymous with pain and suffering. The Bridge of Sighs owes its name to the passage of prisoners, who crossed it when they were taken from the court to prison, as it links the **Doges' Palace**, the seat of the courts of law, with the **Prisons**, built in the 16th century. Justice in Venice was apparently ruthless and, often, summary, so that it is not difficult to imagine the sighs of the prisoners, who were not infrequently jailed

The Bridge of Sighs.

unjustly. It was sufficient for there to be an anonymous report for the Council of Ten to start their investigations. The Bridge of Sighs, built in the 17th century by Antonio Contino from Istrian stone and in the Baroque style, was closed to avoid prisoners trying to escape and allowed a rapid glimpse of the outside world through two open-work windows. It is divided into two separate corridors: one leads to the court and the other to the chambers of the Avogaría (where the lawyers were) and to the

Parlour. The corridors are also linked to the service steps which lead to the terrible cells of the "Piombi", under the roof of the Doges' Palace and to those of the "Pozzi" on the ground floor. The living conditions of the prisoners were truly terrible: they died in their hundreds in the darkness of the tiny and unhealthy cells.

THE CHURCH OF SANTA MARIA DELLA SALUTE

Venice was repeatedly struck by epidemics of the plague, which decimated the population, and the one that devastated the city in 1630 made such an impression that the Senate decided, in

The Church of Santa Maria della Salute seen from the gondola moorings in front of

October of the same year, to invoke the protection of the Virgin Mary, dedicating a new church to her. The place chosen was the present-day Punta della Dogana. This was the beginning of the story of the church of Santa Maria della Salute (St. Mary of Health). A competition was announced and

it was won by a young architect of only 32, Baldassarre Longhena. The solution he adopted was revolutionary for the period: he did not design a classic church with naves, but a monument with an octagonal plan, with the great altar placed in the centre, under a huge dome. Later, the same idea was developed by very fine architects, such as Bernini and Borromini. It took over 50 years to build the monument and Longhena died before he could see it completed. Today the slim dome of Santa Maria della Salute looms up on the horizon when you look at the lagoon from St. Mark's Square: a characteristic part of the skyline of Venice. The church is surmounted by two domes, the larger one of

the Doges' Palace.

which, in the middle, is above the great altar. There are also two bell towers, next to the smaller dome. The interior focuses on the large central volume, dominated by a large vault supported by eight enormous columns. There are six chapels that open up around this. The great altar, designed by Longhena when the building had already started, is decorated with sculptures by the Flemish artist Just Le Court, completed in 1670. Other statues that can be seen in the church are by Bartolomeo Bon, Tullio Lombardo and Gianmaria Morlaiter. There are many pictures, including, by Tiziano *Cosma and Damian* and *Cain and Abel* on the ceiling of the sacristy. Tintoretto painted *The wedding in Cana*, whilst *Jonas and Samson* is by Palma the Younger. There are many canvases by Luca Giordano, including *The Birth of the Virgin Mary*.

Tiziano – Cain murders Abel.

Tiziano - Pentecost.

THE ISLAND OF *St.* GEORGE

The Island of St. George dominated by the bell-tower and the dome.

Small, but rich in history. The Island of St. George the Greater, a few thousand square metres right in front of St. Mark's Square, was for a long time a place of representation for the government of the Serenissima, which enjoyed welcoming here its most illustrious guests. However, the island is believed to have been inhabited as early as Roman times. In 982, the Benedictines founded a monastery there. Today the island is an impor-

Carpaccio – St. George killing the dragon.

tant cultural centre, and hosts the **Giorgio Cini Foundation**, which organizes exhibitions and events of a high level. The Foundation is based in the old **Monastery of St. George**. Nearby is the **Teatro Verde**, where performances in the open-air are held. If you decide to visit the island, you cannot miss going into the Church of St. George the Greater, designed and built by Andrea Palladio (1565-1576), but completed by Scamozzi to the drawings of the master (1610). The beautiful

Tintoretto – a detail of The Last Supper.

dome gives the island its unmistakeable appearance, but it was also designed to give great luminosity to the interior. The brightness is accentuated by the material used, white Istrian stone. The choir is decorated with superb canvases by Tintoretto: *Collecting manna*, on the left wall and the *Last Supper*, on the right wall. In the adjoining chamber of the conclave there is an altar piece from 1516 by Carpaccio showing *St. George killing the dragon*.

A GLIMPSE
OF THE CANALS

The beauty of Venice, the same all year round and in all weathers, lies not only in its monuments and extraordinary palaces.

All of the scenery is absolutely amazing and it can be appreciated even more by strolling through the calles, in the **"sestieri"**, i.e. the six districts of the city: **Cannaregio**, **Castello**, **San Marco**,

A view of a small canal, in a quiet corner of Venice.

San Polo, **Dorsoduro** and **Santa Croce**. You can use the vaporettos to move from one point to another and also reach the less famous places, but where you can observe at first hand the life of the Venetians. On foot, you can come across, for example, one of the now very rare "scueri", the shipyards where the gondolas are built.

Or observe how deliveries are

made to shops, all on wide barges, on the canals.

Every corner can be an unforgettable photo or hide a small shop where you can make unique purchases. from glass to decorated paper and papier maché masks.

THE *H*ISTORICAL REGATTA AND THE CARNIVAL

Amongst the many events that make Venice lively, two in particular have the flavour of tradition: the Carnival and the Historical Regatta. The former is also synonymous with the freedom of customs and thought which characterized the government of the Serenissima. Once, the Carnival lasted much longer and even began on the first Sunday in

A moment of the Historical Regatta which is held every year on the first Sunday in

October, becoming more intense after Epiphany and reaching a climax on Shrove Thursday. It allowed the Venetians of every class to annul their social differences behind their disguises and pranks. The practice of this celebration came back into fashion in 1980, although it is now limited to the traditional days of the present-day Carnival. The first regattas date back to the 13th century,

but after the fall of the Serenissima, they were abolished and were resumed in 1841. Since then, the Historical Regatta has been held on the first Sunday in September and rowers from each district compete against each other in the different rowing techniques.It evokes the celebrations on the water of the golden age of Venice, when the city's vessels sailed behind the Bucintoro, the very precious ceremonial vessel of the doge. The route winds along the Grand Canal. Other regattas are held in the lagoon in the summer. The Carnival and the Historical Regatta are unforgettable experiences.

September on the Grand Canal.

THE ISLAND OF BURANO

Piazza Galluppi, the only square in Burano, with the leaning bell tower of St. Martin.

Burano is an island in the Venetian lagoon, about 6 miles north-east of the city, and densely inhabited by about 3,000 people. It is well known for its colourful houses and for lace-making, which has made it famous all over the world. Tradition has it that it was founded in the period of the invasions of the barbarians, and became one of the six gates of Venice, the "Boreana" (hence the name Burano), thus called because in was positioned in the direction of the Bora, the strong wind that frequently blows over the Lagoon. Burano is small and is

easy to get around. The most impressive thing are the bright colours of the houses. Apparently the colours were used to accurately define the boundaries of property and perhaps also to help the fishermen when, on returning from the sea, they could identify their homes on days of thick fog.

When you get off the vaporetto in a grassy area, you take the "rive" which lead to the main street and then to Piazza Galluppi, the only one in Burano, obtained in ancient times when a canal was filled in. In the square you can visit the **Church of St. Martin Bishop** where, amongst other paintings, there is a canvas by Gian Battista Tiepolo. The bell-tower that looms above it, the only one on the island, leans to one side, due to the subsidence of one side of the foundations, which, as in Venice, are on wooden piles. Next to the church there is the **Chapel of St. Barbara**. In the many small shops, you can

A lace shop in a typical house.

admire the ladies who make the famous lace, using the bobbin method, historically introduced from the 16th century. Lastly, you should not miss the "bussolai", the typical local confectionery, made from eggs, flour and butter.

THE ISLAND OF TORCELLO

Just north of Burano, Torcello is an island in the Lagoon which had a flourishing past and, up to the 16th century, was a prosperous city with tens of thousands of inhabitants. Today there are still some monuments of the splendid city, such as the **Cathedral of Santa Maria Asssunta**, of the 7th century, with a beautiful Byzantine mosaic of the *Last Judgement*, or the 11th century **Church of Santa Fosca**, with a characteristic Greek cross plan.

The Palazzo del Podestà, which is the seat of a rich archaeological museum should also be visited.

The bridge of the Devil.

An aerial view of the Island of Torcello.

THE ƎIDO

The Lido of Venice, in the past the residence of writers like Byron and Thomas Mann.

Extending for 11 km between the Lagoon and the Adriatic, the Lido is an island rich in attractions, including the **Casino** and the **Museum of the Cinema**, where the Venice *Film Festival* is held. The 18th century "murazzi", a dam built to defend the shores from the sea's erosion, are spectacular and run along the coastline of the Alberoni to the square of the Casino. There are many Art Nouveau buildings and parks in the inner streets. The centre of Santa Maria Elisabetta and the riviera San Nicolò with the fortification of the Ridotto are also worth visiting.

THE ISLAND OF MURANO

Famous all over the world for glass-making, Murano is an island in the Lagoon, north-east of Venice with over 5,000 inhabitants and covering 5 small islands. It has been the centre of the Venetian glass industry since the 13th century, when the workshops were all moved here to reduce the risk of fire in the Serenissima. Worth visiting are the **Museum of Glass** in Palazzo Giustinian, the **Basilica of** **St. Mary and St. Donato** and the churches of **St. Mary of the Angels** and **St. Peter Martyr**.

A typical rio of Murano.

RICE WITH PEAS
Risi e bisi

add the rest of the butter and grated Parmesan. After stirring well, taking care that the consistency is neither too liquid nor too thick, place in a soup tureen and serve very hot.

Ingredients for 4 people:

- *200 g Vialone nano rice*
- *1 litre meat stock*
- *1 kg fresh peas*
- *50 g butter*
- *40 g pancetta or ham*
- *1 small onion*
- *3 tablespoons of grated Parmesan*
- *a few sprigs of parsley*
- *salt and pepper*

This is one of the most traditional and tasty dishes of Venetian cuisine. Shell, wash and drain the peas. Put half the butter, all the pancetta (or ham) in a pan and brown for a few minutes and then add the peas. Leave them to absorb the flavours, stirring with a wooden spoon and adding a little hot stock. When half cooked. add the rest of the stock and bring to the boil, then pour in the rice. Continue stirring gently until the rice is cooked, which must be "al dente". Season with salt and pepper,

BUCKWHEAT PASTA WITH DUCK
Bìgoi in tòcio de anara

Clean the duck well, remove the giblets which you will reserve for the sauce and wipe it with a damp cloth. Put the bird in a pan

with salted water, a peeled onion, celery. carrot and bring to the boil until the duck is well cooked.

Then remove the duck from the pan and reserve; you can serve it as a delicious main course together with sauces and vegetables. To prepare the sauce, put the oil and butter in a frying pan and brown the sage leaves and duck giblets.

When they are golden brown, sprinkle with the wine, season with salt and pepper and cook. In the meantime bring the duck stock to the boil, throw in the pasta, cook it and drain. Then dress it with the sauce and sprinkle this flavoursome traditional dish generously with grated Parmesan.

Ingredients for 4 people:

- *400 g bigoli (buckwheat pasta) or*
- *spaghetti*
- *1 medium-sized musk duck*
- *1 onion*
- *1 stalk of celery*
- *1 carrot*
- *3 tablespoons of extra virgin olive oil*
- *30 g butter*
- *½ glass of dry white wine*
- *a few sage leaves grated Parmesan*
- *salt and pepper*

CREAMED DRIED SALT COD

Bacaeà mantecà

Wash the dried salt cod, remove skin and bones and boil it for about five minutes.
Then drain it, chop it finely, place in a pan and pour a glass of milk or thin cream over it.
Season with salt and cook over a very low heat, stirring with a wooden spoon.
When the cod has completely absorbed the milk and has become creamy, pour over two glasses of oil, a little at a time, continuing to fold in with the spoon. In the end it should have the appearance of a soft cream which you can serve, accompanied by slices of toasted polenta, as a very flavoursome main course.

Ingredients for 6 people:

- *1 kg soaked dried salt cod*
- *1 glass of milk or thin cream*
- *2 glasses of extra virgin olive oil*
- *salt*

Editorial conception:
Casa Editrice RotalSele srl
Via Cascina Belcasule, 8
20141 Milano - Italia
e-mail: rotalsele@rotalsele.com

Publishing Editor:
Ermanno Stucchi

Text:
Riccardo Oldani
Daniela Santori

Graphic design and makeup:
Alberto Grazioli

Photographs:
The photographs belong the the Photographic Archives
of the Casa Editrice Rotalsele.

Property of Cartography:
RotalSele srl - Milan

© Copyright 2009
Printed in Italy
by RotalSele srl - Milan
February 2020